THE DINOSAUR COLORING BOOK

THE DINOSAUR COLORING BOOK

Anthony Rao

Dover Publications, Inc.
New York

Frontispiece: A late Cretaceous plant-eater, **Triceratops** had a skull that was 9 feet long, about one-quarter the length of his body. Above the eye sockets were two horns, which were formidable weapons of defense against flesh-eating (carnivorous) dinosaurs, such as Tyrannosaurus. A short nasal horn protruded above the beak-like mouth. The vulnerable neck region was protected by a bony frill at the rear of the skull. For another picture of Triceratops, see page 45.

Copyright © 1980 by Anthony Rao.
All rights reserved under Pan American and International Copyright Conventions.

Published in Canada by General Publishing Company, Ltd., 30 Lesmill Road, Don Mills, Toronto, Ontario.

The Dinosaur Coloring Book is a new work, first published by Dover Publications, Inc., in 1980.

DOVER *Pictorial Archive* SERIES

International Standard Book Number 0-486-24022-3

Manufactured in the United States of America
Dover Publications, Inc.
31 East 2nd Street
Mineola, N.Y. 11501

PUBLISHER'S NOTE

Dinosaurs dominated the earth during the Mesozoic Era, 225 to 65 million years ago. The Mesozoic Era is subdivided into three periods, the Triassic (225 to 193 million years ago), the Jurassic (193 to 136 million years ago) and the Cretaceous (136 to 65 million years ago). Considering the fact that humankind has only been on the earth for the last million years, 150 million years of dinosaurian evolution is an enormous length of time.

The dinosaurs were members of a larger group of reptiles called *archosaurs*, which means "ruling reptiles." Most members of this group, including the dinosaurs, became extinct at the end of the Mesozoic Era. Dinosaurs are known to us today through fossil remains that have been unearthed and studied during the last 150 years. The only archosaurs still alive are the crocodiles, who can provide us with a faint idea of what dinosaurs must have been like. Though unrelated evolutionarily, other modern-day animals give us clues to dinosaur structure and life style. Elephants help us to understand how the legs of huge dinosaurs, such as Brontosaurus, could be structured to support great weight. Rhinoceroses are reminiscent of Triceratops and other horned dinosaurs called ceratopsians.

One of the reasons that dinosaurs are so interesting to study is that so much mystery surrounds them and their habits. Since we have only the evidence of the bones to go by, many important issues are unresolved. For many years experts have debated whether all dinosaurs were cold-blooded, or whether some or all of them were warm-blooded. It is still a mystery why the dinosaurs became extinct. One theory holds that flowering plants developed poisons which killed the herbivorous (plant-eating) dinosaurs. With no herbivores to feed on, the carnivorous (meat-eating) dinosaurs also died. Another theory suggests that a plague-like epidemic wiped them all out. One of the most widely accepted theories maintains that an abrupt climatic change made the earth uninhabitable to dinosaurs.

This book contains drawings, rendered for coloring, of 32 dinosaurs, 6 non-dinosaurian archosaurs, 1 fossil bird and 1 ancient sea turtle. The sequence of the illustrations parallels approximately the development of the dinosaurs; that is, the first plates show the earliest dinosaurs and the last plates show dinosaurs from the end of the Mesozoic Era. (The non-dinosaurs are Dimetrodon, Edaphosaurus, Archaeopteryx, Rhamphorhynchus, Pteranodon, Elasmosaurus, Tylosaurus and Archelon.) Captions contain information of interest about the creatures depicted: size, habitat, classification, related dinosaurs, means of defense or offense, skeletal structure and evolutionary significance. Color renderings of some dinosaurs are shown on the covers, but no one really knows what colors they were, so don't be afraid to use your imagination. It is our hope that this book will not only provide hours of coloring pleasure, but will also give you an introduction to the study of dinosaurs and related prehistoric animals. You will find many excellent books about these fascinating creatures in your local library. In addition, many large cities in the United States and Canada have natural history museums that display fossilized remains of dinosaurs.

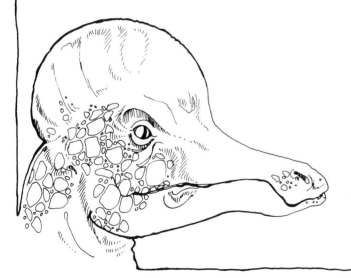

ALPHABETICAL LIST OF DINOSAURS

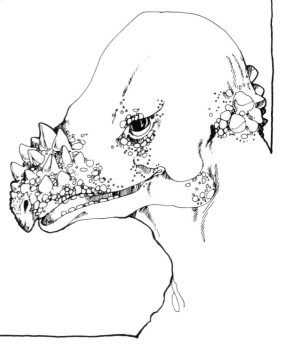

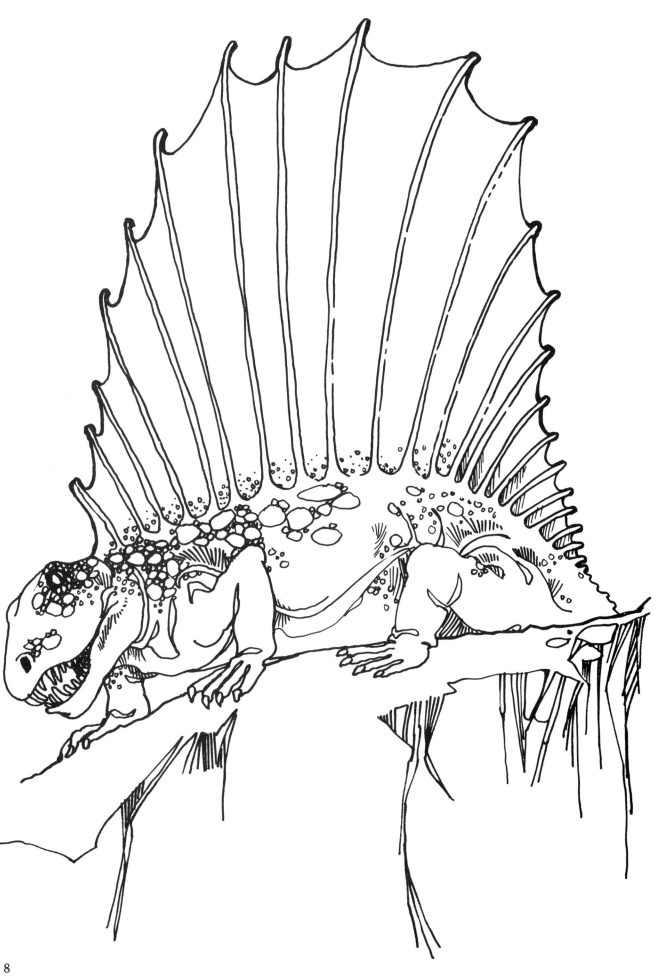

DIMETRODON (left) and **EDAPHOSAURUS** (above) were primitive lizards that lived during the late Permian Period (just preceding the Mesozoic Era). They both possessed a sail, which stretched the length of their backs and helped to regulate body temperature. When too cold, they would turn broadside to the sun to absorb heat. Both were carnivorous. Dimetrodon was about 11 feet long and lived in what is now Texas. Edaphosaurus was slightly smaller and lived mainly in swampy areas, where he fed on shellfish.

PROCOMPSOGNATHUS (below) lived during the Triassic Period and belonged to a group of primitive early dinosaurs called *coelosaurs*. These dinosaurs were small and nimble carnivores, and could run very rapidly on their hind legs. Procompsognathus ("first pretty jaw") was only 3 feet long and had three-toed, birdlike feet. Remains of this dinosaur have been found in southern Germany. **PLATEOSAURUS** (right), whose name means "flat lizard," was a herbivore who measured 20 feet in length. He is thought to be a Triassic-age ancestor to the much larger *sauropod* dinosaurs such as Brontosaurus and Brachiosaurus. He normally walked on all four legs, but would rear up on his hind legs to feed.

Large by Triassic Period standards, **TERATOSAURUS** (left), whose name means "awesome lizard," was a ferocious carnivore who was 20 feet long and weighed nearly three-quarters of a ton. He had a very large skull and hands with large, curved claws, which were excellent for slashing and grasping. Many paleontologists believe Teratosaurus to be an early ancestor of Tyrannosaurus. **COELOPHYSIS** (above), like Procompsognathus, was a Triassic coelosaur with an elongated head filled with fine, sharp teeth for tearing flesh. Coelophysis ("hollow form") was 8 feet long and 3 feet high but weighed only 40 pounds, partly as a result of having lightweight, hollow bones. The remains of a large group of these dinosaurs found in New Mexico indicate that they might have been cannibals, like modern-day crocodiles.

ARCHAEOPTERYX ("ancient wing") is the earliest fossil bird known, dating from the Jurassic Period. Because it had many dinosaurian features, such as sharp teeth and a long bony tail, many experts believe it to be descended from the coelosaurs. In fact, it may be an evolutionary "missing link" between reptiles and birds. Archeopteryx had stumpy wings with feathers, and probably was capable of only short bursts of flight. It was about the size of a modern crow.

ORNITHOLESTES (also called Coelurus) was one of the largest coelosaurs, somewhat larger than a man, but not nearly as heavy. He was capable of great speed and had sharp, hooked claws. Ornitholestes ("bird robber") lived during the Jurassic Period, and is thought to have fed upon small reptiles and early birds, such as Archeopteryx.

COMPSOGNATHUS ("pretty jaw") was one of the smallest dinosaurs that ever lived, with a total length of only about 2 feet. He lived during the late Triassic Period and is classified as a coelosaur, like Procompsognathus, Coelophysis and Ornitholestes. Compsognathus had three-fingered claws for grasping and tearing the flesh of small lizards, upon which he fed.

An early *pterosaur* ("winged reptile"), **RHAMPHORHYNCHUS**
lived during the middle Jurassic Period. He had paper-thin wings,
the outer portions of which were supported by the extended finger
bones of the tiny hands seen on top of the wings. Rhamphorhynchus ("prow beak") was about 2 feet long, and probably glided
more often than he flew, since his flight muscles were very weak.
The long tail, thickened and flattened at the end, served as a
rudder.

ALLOSAURUS (left), a late Jurassic carnivore, was an ancestor of Tyrannosaurus. He attained a length of 40 feet and had enormous jaws with razor-sharp teeth. He used these teeth to feed upon the great vegetarian dinosaurs of this period, such as Brontosaurus and Diplodocus. Allosaurus' skull (above) consisted of many flexible arches, with large openings between them. This design made the skull lighter and may have permitted it to expand when the dinosaur gulped down huge chunks of flesh. Allosaurus means "different lizard."

CAMPTOSAURUS (above and right) belonged to a group of dinosaurs that first flourished during the Jurassic Period, called *ornithopod,* or "bird-hipped" dinosaurs. These dinosaurs had bird-like pelvises and horny beaks, used for eating plants. Ornithopods normally ambled along on four legs, but could stand on two for the purposes of feeding or running away from predators. Camptosaurus ("bent lizard") was a small dinosaur, being only 5 to 10 feet in length. He had hoof-like feet and hands, which were useful for pulling and holding foliage, but were useless for defense.

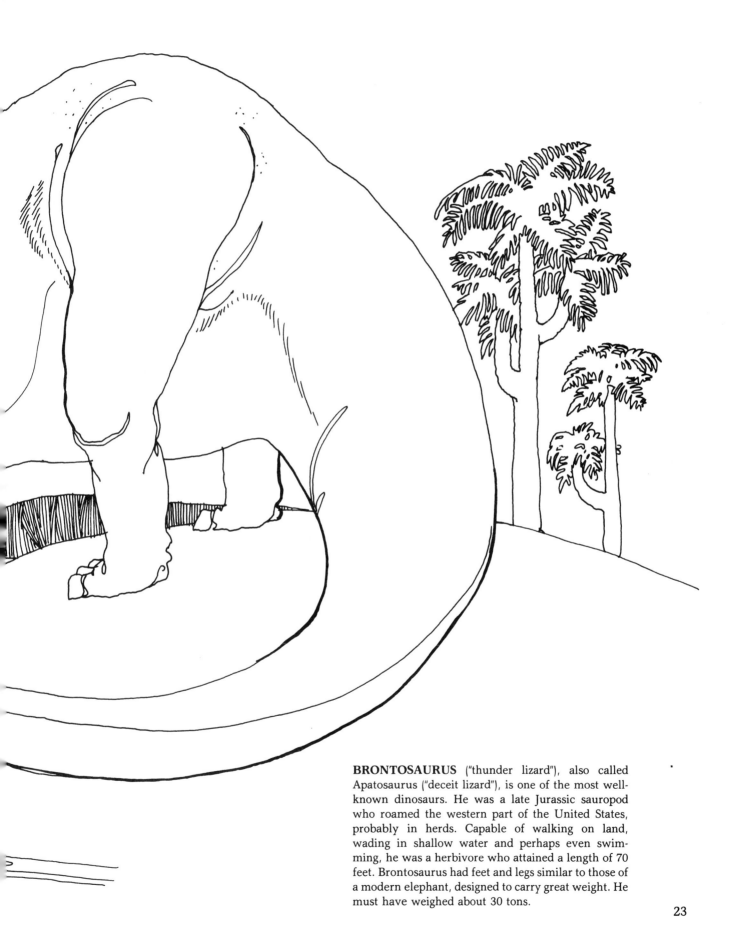

BRONTOSAURUS ("thunder lizard"), also called Apatosaurus ("deceit lizard"), is one of the most well-known dinosaurs. He was a late Jurassic sauropod who roamed the western part of the United States, probably in herds. Capable of walking on land, wading in shallow water and perhaps even swimming, he was a herbivore who attained a length of 70 feet. Brontosaurus had feet and legs similar to those of a modern elephant, designed to carry great weight. He must have weighed about 30 tons.

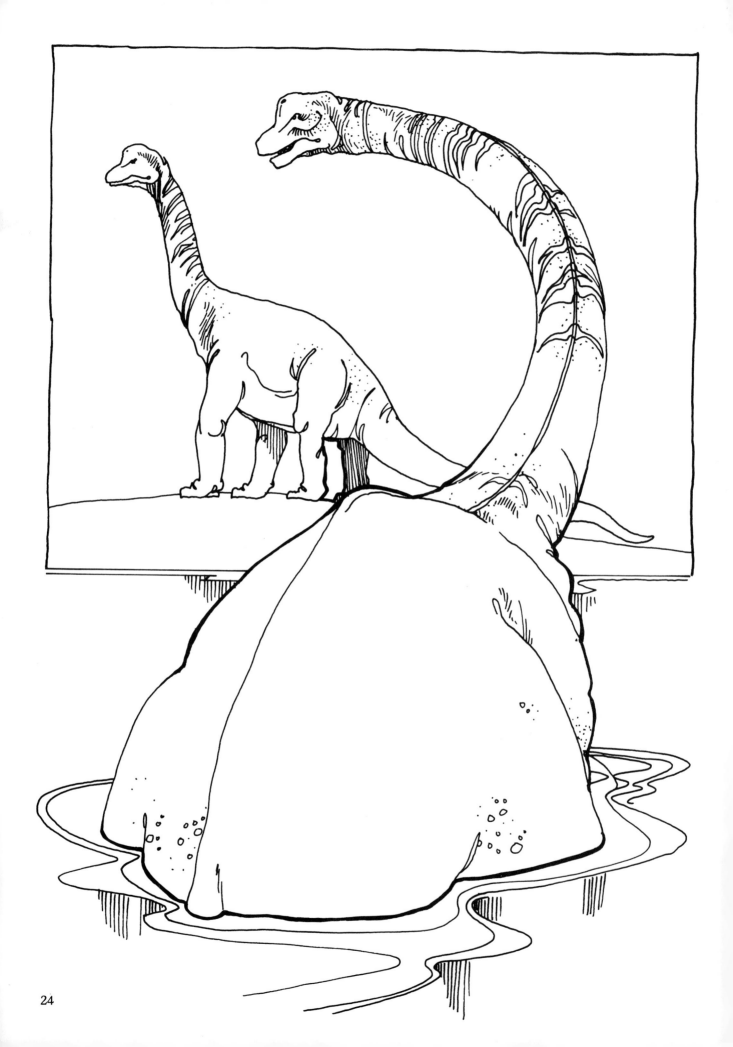

Living during the late Jurassic Period, **BRACHIOSAURUS** (left) belonged to a group of dinosaurs called *sauropods*. These dinosaurs shared many characteristics with modern-day lizards, such as five-toed feet. Brachiosaurus ("arm lizard") was possibly the largest animal that ever lived; some skeletons are 100 feet long, indicating that the creature must have weighed more than 50 tons. Brachiosaurus had larger front legs than hind legs, an unusual feature. The Brachiosaurus skull (above) had nostrils and eye sockets placed very high up, which has led many experts to believe that he spent much of his time in the water, browsing land and underwater plants with his long neck.

STEGOSAURUS (above and left) roamed North America during the Jurassic Age in large numbers. He was the size of a big automobile, and had a double row of bony plates running the entire length of his back and tail. These plates protected Stegosaurus from the marauding carnivores of the period, such as Allosaurus. Additional protection was furnished by four pointed spikes arranged at the end of his muscular tail. Stegosaurus ("shingle lizard") was a plant eater and had a beak-like mouth lined with small, dull teeth. The brain of Stegosaurus was the size of a peanut.

PROTOCERATOPS (left) was one of the earliest members of a group of dinosaurs called *ceratopsians*, which arose during Cretaceous times. This group was characterized by a relatively enormous skull with a parrot-like beak. The skull extended backward into a bony frill, which protected the neck and furnished a point of attachment for powerful jaw muscles. These muscles enabled the ceratopsians (who were herbivores) to crop the toughest foliage. Protoceratops ("first horned face") was 6 feet long and weighed about 400 pounds. Many skeletons and eggs of this dinosaur have been found in Mongolia.
OVIRAPTOR (above) was a Cretaceous coelosaur who measured only 3 feet in length. He is related to earlier coelosaurs, such as Coelophysis and Campsognathus. Oviraptor means "egg stealer." He got this name because his skeleton was first found among a nest of Protoceratops eggs in Mongolia.

ELASMOSAURUS ("ribbon reptile") belonged to a group of marine reptiles, called *plesio-saurs,* who lived in late Cretaceous times. He had a 20-foot-long neck comprised of 76 vertebrae, which was capable of catching fish with quick, powerful stabs. Elasmosaurus was 40 feet long overall, and had four paddles for swimming.

TYLOSAURUS was a late Cretaceous marine lizard who measured 20 feet in length. He belonged to a group of similar lizards who left the land during early Cretaceous times and took to the sea. These lizards, called *mososaurs*, fed on fish and mollusks. They swam by means of their strong tails, using their appendages as rudders.

PTERANODON (left) was a pterosaur ("winged lizard") who lived in the cliffs surrounding the warm shallow seas that covered much of North America during the late Cretaceous Period. He had a wingspan of 27 feet, but lacked the flight muscles for strong, flapping flight. As a result, he depended on breezes and updrafts to propel him over the water like a glider. His pointed beak was useful for spearing fish. Pteranodon means "winged and toothless." **ARCHELON** (above) was the largest turtle of all time, measuring 12 feet in length. He lived during the late Cretaceous Period and was the ancestor of the modern Galapagos sea turtle. Archelon's heavy armor protected him from attack by seagoing predators of the period, such as Elasmosaurus and Tylosaurus.

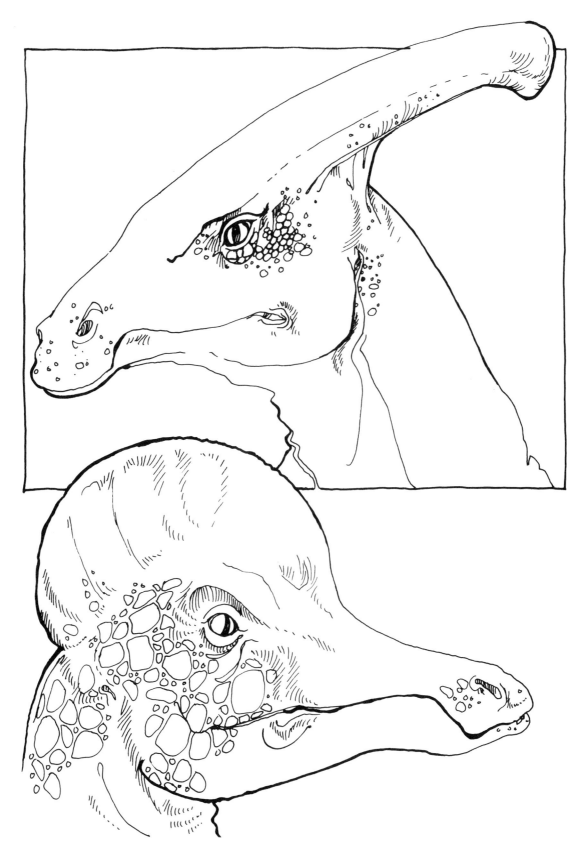

ANATOSAURUS (left) belonged to a group of late Cretaceous dinosaurs called *hadrosaurs*. This group was characterized by pebbly skin, duck-like bills and bony head crests in a variety of odd shapes. Other members of this group include **PARASAUROLOPHUS** (top) and **CORYTHOSAURUS** (bottom). Hadrosaurs were herbivores; their mouths often contained nearly 2000 small teeth for grinding tough foliage. They lacked an effective means of defense against predators, but were exceptionally fast runners and swimmers. The purpose of the hollow head crest remains a mystery. The most interesting theory holds that it served as a resonator to amplify mating calls. Anatosaurus ("duck lizard") was 40 feet long; Parasaurolophus, 30 feet long and Corythosaurus ("helmet lizard"), 25 feet long.

GORGOSAURUS ("gorgon lizard") was a 35-foot-long carnivore who lived in middle Cretaceous times in the region of Alberta, Canada. A close cousin of Tyrannosaurus, he had powerful jaws equipped with sharp teeth for tearing flesh. His jaws were his only weapon, since his tiny, two-fingered hands lacked the strength for combat. Gorgosaurus was clumsy and could not move very rapidly; he must have made quite a racket crashing through the underbrush in pursuit of victims.

PACHYCEPHALOSAURUS was an ornithopod dinosaur (like Camptosaurus) who lived in late Cretaceous times. He had a skull that was 2 feet long and covered with ugly bumps. His skull was also 9 inches thick, which has led many experts to speculate that males butted heads during mating season like modern-day sheep and goats. Pachycephalosaurus ("thick-headed reptile") grazed for vegetation in herds, and inhabited territories that are now Mongolia, England and the western United States.

ANKYLOSAURUS (above), more correctly called Euoplocephalus, was a late Cretaceous herbivore whose body was covered with heavy armor plates, like a tank. He was 15 feet long and weighed about four times as much as most dinosaurs his size. A narrow row of spikes projected from both sides of his body. His tail ended in a huge bony club, which could be swung at attackers. Ankylosaurus means "stiff lizard." **LAMBEOSAURUS** (right) was a late Cretaceous hadrosaur with an unusually shaped bony crest. Related dinosaurs include Anatosaurus, Parasaurolophus and Corythosaurus. The remains of all of these hadrosaurs have been found in great abundance in Alberta, Canada. Lambeosaurus, named after paleontologist L. M. Lambe, was 30 feet long.

ORNITHOMIMUS belonged to a group of Cretaceous coelosaurs popularly called "ostrich dinosaurs." He was similar in size and habits to the modern ostrich. He had hollow bones and long hind legs, perfectly suited for fast running. His jaws were beak-like, with no teeth. Ornithomimus ("bird mimic") was probably omnivorous, eating insects and little lizards as well as fruits and, especially, eggs.

STYRACOSAURUS was a Cretaceous ceratopsian who was midway, evolutionarily, between Protoceratops and Triceratops. He had a classic ceratopsian bony frill on top of his skull, from which projected six protective horns. Styracosaurus ("spiny lizard") also had a nasal horn and a beak, and measured 18 feet in length.

SPINOSAURUS (left) was a 39-foot-long creature who lived in late Cretaceous Egypt. Much like the Permian lizard Dimetrodon, he had a sail which ran the length of his back, probably acting as a sort of radiator. The spines on this sail were as long as 6 feet. **DEINONYCHUS** (above) was first discovered in the early Cretaceous rocks of Montana. He was a coelosaur (hence, a carnivore) who measured 9 feet in length, and must have been a very swift runner. Deinonychus had a unique weapon: the second toe of each foot had a huge, sickle-shaped claw that remained off the ground. When he kicked his leg backwards, this claw could rake across a foe with tremendous force. Deinonychus means "terrible claw."

TYRANNOSAURUS (left) was the fiercest and largest carnivore that ever lived, measuring over 50 feet in length and standing 18 feet tall. He walked rather clumsily in a bent-over position, with his tail raised off the ground for balance. His most formidable weapons were his huge jaws and sharp-clawed hind limbs. His forelimbs were virtually useless in battle. Herbivores of the Cretaceous Age responded to the threat of the giant carnivores by developing better means of defense. **TRICERATOPS** (above), the last and the largest of the ceratopsians, measured 36 feet in length and weighed over 8 tons. His three-horned head was one-quarter the length of his body. His skull possessed the bony frill and beaked mouth characteristic of the ceratopsians. Triceratops means "three-horned face." Even Tyrannosaurus would flee the head-on charge of Triceratops.

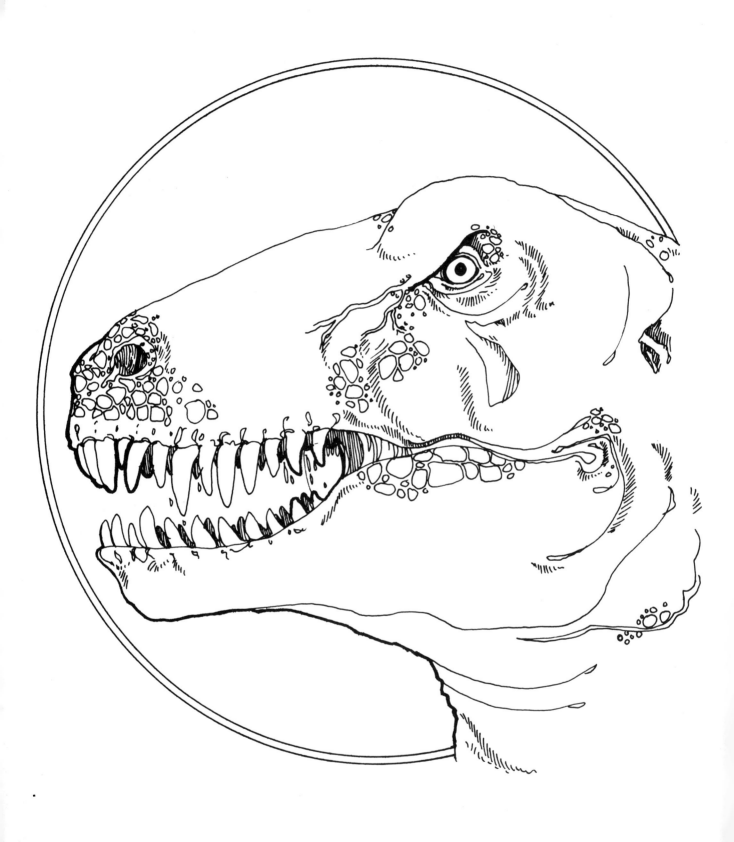

The head of **TYRANNOSAURUS** was 4 feet in length. His teeth were as long as 6 inches, and had serrated edges, like a steak knife. Tyrannosaurus means "tyrant lizard."